# REMOTE WORK

## Pros and Cons of the Changing Workplace

Gail Snyder

San Diego, CA

© 2024 ReferencePoint Press, Inc.
Printed in the United States

**For more information, contact:**
ReferencePoint Press, Inc.
PO Box 27779
San Diego, CA 92198
www.ReferencePointPress.com

ALL RIGHTS RESERVED.
No part of this work covered by the copyright hereon may be reproduced or used in any form or by any means—graphic, electronic, or mechanical, including photocopying, recording, taping, web distribution, or information storage retrieval systems—without the written permission of the publisher.

---

LIBRARY OF CONGRESS CATALOGING-IN-PUBLICATION DATA

Names: Snyder, Gail, author.
Title: Remote work : pros and cons of the changing workplace / by Gail Snyder.
Description: San Diego, CA : ReferencePoint Press, Inc., [2024] | Includes bibliographical references and index.
Identifiers: LCCN 2023019015 (print) | LCCN 2023019016 (ebook) | ISBN 9781678206062 (library binding) | ISBN 9781678206079 (ebook)
Subjects: LCSH: Telecommuting--Juvenile literature. | Flexible work arrangements--Juvenile literature.
Classification: LCC HD2336.3 .S69 2024  (print) | LCC HD2336.3  (ebook) | DDC 658.3/123--dc23/eng/20230421
LC record available at https://lccn.loc.gov/2023019015
LC ebook record available at https://lccn.loc.gov/2023019016

# CONTENTS

**Introduction**     4
A Seismic Shift in the Workplace

**Chapter One**     8
What Is It Like to Work from Home?

**Chapter Two**     19
What Are the Advantages of Working Remotely?

**Chapter Three**     31
What Are the Disadvantages of Remote Work?

**Chapter Four**     43
What Will the Future of Remote Work Look Like?

Source Notes     54
For Further Research     57
Index     59
Picture Credits     63
About the Author     64

# INTRODUCTION

# A Seismic Shift in the Workplace

The COVID-19 epidemic that began in 2020 changed the world virtually overnight. With a sometimes fatal, highly contagious respiratory disease spreading from one human being to another, the pandemic led to massive changes in the way people went to school, shopped for food and other necessities, and conducted their work lives.

While essential workers—including medical professionals, nursing home aides, and food service employees—continued to perform their jobs in person, many employers began allowing their employees to work from home. In the process, employers discovered that employees could be productive even when under separate roofs.

## Work-from-Home Days Skyrocket

The numbers tell the story: before the pandemic struck, remote work accounted for only 5 percent of US workdays, according to WFH Research, the research division of a company that links job seekers to remote job opportunities. But by 2022 the number of work-from-home days had climbed to 30 percent of total workdays.

While that may not seem like a huge increase, Nicholas Bloom, an economics professor at Stanford University in California, puts it in a historical perspective: "It's probably the largest change to US labor markets since World War II, when you had a big increase in female labor force participation."[1] Bloom is referring to the fact that during World War II, as able-bodied men were drafted into the military, many women entered the American workforce for the first time. Motivated by patriotism, they worked in factories and ammunition plants, among other places, performing jobs they had never done before.

Seventy-five years later, some 28 million employees were also doing something most of them had never done before: working from home, according to the US Census Bureau. In some cases, these workers found themselves relying on new technologies that enabled them to do their jobs miles from their former workplaces.

> "It's probably the largest change to US labor markets since World War II, when you had a big increase in female labor force participation."[1]
>
> —Nicholas Bloom, Stanford University economics professor

## Each Story Is Unique

Behind the statistics are the stories of real people whose lives have been greatly impacted by the ability to work remotely. One such story belongs to thirty-three-year-old Amanda Pensack, who works on marketing campaigns for a high-tech company and participates in meetings from her home laptop just as easily as she used to do sitting in a meeting room or in front of a computer in her cubicle at work.

Her remote job allows her to wake up only minutes before she is expected to start work, which is important to her because she finds getting up early a struggle. She is able to do that since she prepares what she needs to be ready the night before. For example, she may review her notes the night before she has a morning meeting with a client. For her, getting rid of a commute was a godsend because she no longer has to give up sleep to eat breakfast or get in her car and arrive at the office before her body is fully awake.

Her new, more personalized schedule makes her happier. "I think [later starts] are becoming more acceptable," she says. "I don't think managers care that much about what time exactly you log on; they care about you getting your work done."[2]

## A Permanent Remote Workforce

As important as remote work is to Pensack and other individual employees, it represents something even greater to Marc Cenedella, chief executive officer (CEO) of Ladders, a New York–based company that provides career news and advice. He says, "The impact of the remote revolution on American life is under-hyped and under-appreciated. As a nation, we are now committed to a

*About 30 percent of all US work is now done remotely. Many remote workers enjoy greater flexibility, including the ability to juggle family and job responsibilities.*

permanently remote workforce. We can't go back and we won't want to. This dramatic change will have a profound impact on careers, families and communities for decades to come."[3]

Julia Pollak, chief economist for the employment marketplace ZipRecruiter, also thinks that remote work is here to stay. "I do think it's hard to put the genie back in the bottle on this one," she says. "Once you hire a remote employee who lives elsewhere—as many companies have—it's very hard to insist that people who live near the office come in all the time."[4]

Major disruptive global events such as wars and pandemics have a way of accelerating change in society and the way people earn their living. Years ago, it was difficult to imagine a world in which women made up a significant portion of the workforce; today it is hard to imagine a world in which some form of remote work does not exist.

> "Once you hire a remote employee who lives elsewhere—as many companies have—it's very hard to insist that people who live near the office come in all the time."[4]
>
> —Julia Pollak, chief economist for ZipRecruiter

## CHAPTER ONE

# What Is It Like to Work from Home?

Although she could probably work in her pajamas, Stella Garber favors leggings and sweaters. When she has a virtual meeting, as she typically does many times a day, she usually applies makeup, too. The Chicago, Illinois, mother of a young child is a marketing expert and team leader—someone who figures out how to sell products by creating materials that address consumers' wants and needs. Working at home, she prefers to carry out her duties from a standing desk.

She starts work at 8:00 a.m. by checking Slack, a message-sharing app that is considered faster, easier, and more secure than email, to see whether there are any issues she needs to address. Then she checks her email. "Relying on digital tools outside of email means while your inbox is never crazy, you still have many other tools to check to see what people need from you. I can barely see my desk because it's so messy,"[5] she says. For meetings, she relies on Zoom, a videoconferencing app that allows her to meet face-to-face virtually with coworkers and clients while also sharing her screen with them to give them access to her company's data.

She says, "In a managerial role at a tech company I'm just as busy as I would be in an office. In fact, I think I'm more busy because I can fit more meetings into my day and get more done without all the distractions."[6] Although her workday usually ends at 4:00 p.m., Garber performs some work after her son goes to sleep. Still, she feels fortunate to be able to see him, however briefly, during work hours.

> "In a managerial role at a tech company I'm just as busy as I would be in an office. In fact, I think I'm more busy because I can fit more meetings into my day and get more done without all the distractions."[6]
>
> —Stella Garber, Chicago-based marketing expert

### Differing Workdays

Meagan Miller's remote work experience is quite a bit different from Garber's. As a customer service representative for Spire, a natural gas company in her hometown of Birmingham, Alabama, Miller's job requires her to wear a headset with a microphone while working her shift from noon to 11:00 p.m. She works at a computer atop a desk located near her couch. Miller is closely monitored by her employer. This includes having to let Spire know when she needs a bathroom break—although sometimes, she admits, she simply does not take one because she worries that too many callers will land in her queue if she even temporarily stops handling them.

She keeps an array of snacks nearby so she can maintain her energy and focus while answering customers' questions and fielding their complaints. Her 5:00 p.m. lunch break, when it finally arrives, lasts only fifteen minutes.

Vivek Nair of San Francisco, California, has more freedom than either Garber or Miller. Before beginning his workday, which largely takes place in his bedroom, he drinks some coffee and meditates to clear his mind in preparation for running Pesto, the company he cofounded. The company offers an app that makes working remotely more seamless for teams in separate locations. The currently free app has been used by more than ten thousand teams.

With no commute to worry about, remote workers can spend their morning time on fulfilling activities such as exercising or enjoying an extra cup of coffee.

Nair reads and responds to customers' emails before 8:30 a.m. and launches his company's software so team members can discuss priorities for the day and feel connected. His mornings are often devoted to online meetings, and on most days he walks to a Chipotle restaurant, where he can grab a quick lunch. He allows forty-five minutes to get there, eat, and return home. In the afternoon, he solves problems that customers are having with his platform, dreams up new features to make the app more useful, and creates marketing materials to gain new customers. He takes a thirty-minute break in the afternoon to catch up on the news before wrapping up his workday at 6:30 p.m.

## A Brief History of Remote Work

Whether they realize it or not, Garber, Miller, Nair, and others who have worked remotely would not have been able to do so were it not for the pioneers who began experimenting with it fifty years ago.

One of those visionaries was Jack Nilles, a scientist for the National Aeronautics and Space Administration, the federal agency that oversees the nation's space program. Nilles is credited with coming up with the concept of telecommuting. This was a word he invented by combining the words *telephone* and *commuting*. To perform such work in the early 1970s when Nilles was studying the concept, all one needed was a landline and a place to conduct business. All landlines are connected by an extensive network of wires and cables that run underground or are strung overhead, telephone pole to telephone pole. Landlines date back to the invention of the telephone by Alexander Graham Bell in 1876 and are still very much in use today. They work by sending voice data over telephone lines, and users must remain attached to the unit to have a conversation.

Several factors piqued Nilles's interest in this new way of working. One was where he lived—Los Angeles, California, a city of freeways in which travel by car is necessary to get anywhere. The second was a gasoline shortage that roiled the United States

## Who Cannot Work Remotely

There are those who are currently shut out of the remote work universe. "It's very hard for you to work remotely if you are a barista in a coffee shop or you're working in a manufacturing plant. The sorts of jobs that people with low education tend to do that require them to be physically present," says Jose Maria Barrero, an economist and founder of a research firm specializing in work-from-home issues. That is why lower-income people do not often have the same remote work opportunities as those who earn more.

Researchers have found that it is harder to find remote work in states where residents have lower incomes and educational attainments. In a 2020 survey of 260,000 Americans taken by the US Census Bureau, fewer than 20 percent of respondents in rural states—Alabama, Arkansas, Kentucky, Louisiana, and Mississippi—reported that someone in their household had worked remotely that week. Average annual income in those households was $48,000 to $56,000. By contrast, in states where the average income was $79,000 to $91,000, at least 35 percent of respondents stated that someone in their household had worked remotely that week.

Quoted in Phillip Reese, "A Work-from-Home Culture Takes Root in California," *Ukiah (CA) Daily Journal*, November 23, 2022. www.ukiahdailyjournal.com.

in 1973 and 1974, leading to long lines at gas pumps and a rapid rise in gasoline prices. Nilles, who has lived long enough to see his idea reach fruition, recalls what he thought at the time: "Most of the traffic was people going from home to work and back. And much of that was people going to their offices, not to factories or other workplaces where they had to be there. When they get to the office, they get on the phone and talk to somebody somewhere else. I said, 'Why don't they just do that from home in the first place?'"[7]

Nilles is credited with conducting one of the first studies on telecommuting. The study followed two thousand employees of a Los Angeles–based insurance company. During a nine-month period, they were allowed to work in small satellite campuses located near their homes. That enabled those employees to reduce the amount of time they spent commuting to work on their city's jam-packed freeways, while also saving them money they would have otherwise spent on gasoline. Moreover, the study subjects reported being more productive, and the insurance company trimmed its maintenance costs for its office. While the study ended up being the subject of a book, it did not lead to any dramatic changes in thinking about remote work—not even for the insurance company that participated in the study. Although Nilles estimated that the company could have saved $5 million a year by continuing the experiment, it chose not to. "That was my early lesson that this was going to be hard to sell," says Nilles. "They're used to business as usual. I've been fighting that ever since."[8]

Three years later, economist Frank W. Schiff wrote an article for the *Washington Post* in which he championed telecommuting. In this well-received piece, he imagined a future in which more people would work outside the office:

> Millions of Americans commute to work five days a week, primarily by car or bus, in a massive population movement which accounts for much of the country's gasoline consumption, traffic congestion and air pollution, and which

is a major source of mental and physical stress. There are many possible ways to ameliorate these problems, but, surprisingly, virtually no attention has been paid to the contribution which could be made by working at home one or two days a week. While only a minority of workers would be able to use this option, their impact on reducing gasoline use and alleviating other conditions related to commuting could be quite pronounced. Moreover, the size of such a group could increase rapidly and substantially in the next few years.[9]

Like Nilles, Schiff was responsible for creating a new word that soon found its way into the collective vocabulary. "Flexiplace" expanded the idea of remote work to include working from many different types of spaces, including coworking spaces, satellite offices, and anywhere an employee chooses to work, including home.

*Cars clog Interstate 405 near Los Angeles, California. Automobile commuters account for much of America's gasoline consumption, traffic congestion, and air pollution.*

## High-Tech Companies Led the Way

While most companies were not paying much attention to the ideas of Nilles or Schiff, some high-tech companies were. This is not surprising, given that such companies earn their profits by anticipating trends and supplying the technology needed to effect them. The tech companies IBM, Cisco, and Sun Microsystems were among the earliest companies to implement remote work.

In 1983 five employees working at IBM were given some unexpected news that would place them at the forefront of employment history. As part of an experiment, the corporation that began life as International Business Machines—which went into business a century ago manufacturing products such as electric typewriters and personal calculators—permitted these employees to work from home using remote computer terminals it provided. The experiment succeeded well enough that the company kept adding more remote employees. By 2009, 40 percent of IBM workers, representing about 144,000 people in more than 170 countries, were working remotely.

## A Boon for Workers with Disabilities

Some individuals have physical or mental conditions that would make it difficult for them to commute to and work in an office. For people like Tracy S. of Clemmons, South Carolina, the ability to work remotely was life changing. Tracy is a nurse with a rare illness that makes it difficult for her to walk and threatens her ability to work in her profession. Luckily for Tracy, the health insurance company Humana hired her to work as a full-time remote care manager, responsible for checking on subscribers to make sure they are receiving the health care they need to remain as healthy and independent as possible. Tracy said that remote work "impacts my life in every conceivable way! . . . I can work full-time and contribute to society. I do not have to worry about finding someone to drive me to work. I can continue to utilize 22 years of nursing experience. . . . Even when my legs are hurting or frozen up, it does not stop me from walking across the hallway to my office and sitting down to work."

Quoted in Rachel Pelta, "Success Stories: 30 People Share How Flexibility Has Changed Their Lives," FlexJobs. www.flexjobs.com.

Beginning a full ten years after IBM started its experiment, Cisco's program allowed employees to connect to work through personal computers via wireless routers that pick up and send signals from a network of underground cables. Cisco makes equipment that allows computers to share data, printers, and other devices.

Meanwhile, at Sun Microsystems, employees were given the option to work from home in the late 1990s. Before it was acquired in 2010 and ceased to exist, Sun Microsystems sold computer workstations, servers, and software.

These impactful experiments at three different companies produced results that could be compared. Some of the most striking related to the reduced need for office space. The average office worker requires 150 to 157 square feet (13.9 to 14.6 sq. m) in an office building. In 2009 IBM was able to reduce its office space enough to save $100 million a year; it finally ended its remote program after thirty-four years.

Only three years into its program, Cisco executives reported saving $195 million and observing greater productivity among its workforce. For Sun Microsystems, which made remote work an option for 35 percent of its employees, the reported savings over a decade were half a billion dollars, money saved in part by fewer expenditures for office space.

## Onboarding of the Federal Government

One entity that has a large real estate presence and therefore an interest in achieving cost savings through remote work is America's largest employer, the federal government. The agency that oversees the buildings it owns and leases is the General Services Administration, which is responsible for supervising and maintaining over 371 million square feet (34.5 million sq. m) of space in eighty-six hundred buildings spread among more than twenty-two hundred communities.

Not surprisingly, then, the federal government played an important part in the evolution of remote work, culminating in Congress's passage of the Telework Enhancement Act in 2010.

The act was created to make remote work easier for federal employees who wanted to have the option. Among other things, the act, signed into law during the administration of President Barack Obama, set up formal policies allowing federal employees to work remotely without being penalized and created standards and expectations for remote work, along with training programs for employees and their supervisors. Today federal employees eligible to work remotely may work up to eight days every two weeks at a remote location.

## Who Can Work Remotely

Over the years, the federal government has earned more of a reputation for making changes at a slow pace than for its innovation as an employer. But the fact that even federal agencies like the US Food and Drug Administration, which regulates the sale of pharmaceuticals and medical devices, are willing to let employees do their work remotely attests to how widely accepted the practice is becoming.

As remote work became more widespread, the kinds of jobs able to be performed remotely also expanded. Human resources director Samantha Lambert of Centific, a digital and technology services company, says, "Ten years ago [in the 2010s], remote employment basically meant a telemarketing or customer service position at below minimum wage. It was rarely connected with a full-time career. Now technology affords us the ability to get the same job done, no matter

> "Ten years ago [in the 2010s], remote employment basically meant a telemarketing or customer service position at below minimum wage. It was rarely connected with a full-time career. Now technology affords us the ability to get the same job done, no matter where in the world we are. [It has] enabled us to be in contact with co-workers or clients at any time."[10]
>
> —Samantha Lambert, human resources director of Centific

*Some high-touch jobs, including hairdressing, cannot be done remotely. Many low-touch desk jobs, however, can be very efficiently done on a remote basis.*

where in the world we are. [It has] enabled us to be in contact with co-workers or clients at any time."[10]

One group that seems to have benefited the most from remote work is managers. Gusto, a payroll and human resources app for small businesses, has reported that supervisors are more likely to work remote jobs than those they manage. Furthermore, people who work in certain industries—technology, communications, finance, insurance, and professional services—are more likely to take advantage of the remote option. Says author Tsedal Neeley, "If we leave out the high-touch jobs such as hair salons or tattoo parlors, many jobs thrive in a remote format—especially those that require deep problem-solving and undistracted concentration. Software engineers, graphic designers, editors, writers or other workers who can do more of their work at a computer fit that category."[11]

## Nilles Has the Last Laugh

While not everyone has the ability to work remotely, it is increasingly possible to do so in the fifty years since Jack Nilles became the father of telework. He has lived long enough to see how useful and common the concept could be. He has joked that it only took him forty-eight years to be an overnight success, with the rest of the world finally catching up to him. Yet even he recognizes that what it is like to work remotely is something that will continue to evolve. "We're still in the middle of a giant experiment. . . . My original objective in 1973 was to see if this is feasible in a contemporary American business environment. Now, it's clearly feasible. Now we have to go in and figure out what else does all this mean."[12] That is the task companies large and small, in the United States and abroad, face in the 2020s.

> "My original objective in 1973 was to see if this is feasible in a contemporary American business environment. Now, it's clearly feasible. Now we have to go in and figure out what else does all this mean."[12]
>
> —Jack Nilles, the father of telework

## CHAPTER TWO

# What Are the Advantages of Working Remotely?

When it comes to accruing the benefits of remote work, few people can beat the experience of Rhiannon Cook, a thirty-four-year-old marketing professional who spent five years reveling in the freedom of working from anywhere while traveling as a "digital nomad."

Thanks to her skills as a marketer and her affinity for working for start-up companies that are perfectly attuned to having remote workers, Cook's experiences with remote work have gone well. It has allowed her to earn money and see the world. She has worked in and visited countries in Europe such as Germany, Hungary, and Denmark; in Asia, such as Vietnam, Thailand, and Japan; in South America, such as Chile, Peru, and Colombia; and in Africa, such as Kenya and Rwanda.

Before switching to remote work, she was a full-time in-person employee of a Pittsburgh, Pennsylvania, advertising agency. Since one of her clients was based in

Travel-loving remote workers can do their jobs just as easily from anywhere—even a tiny village like Santa Fiora, Italy (shown). As long as there is an internet connection, they can work.

Atlanta, Georgia, she was required to fly to that city several times a month, sometimes for just a single day. Occasionally, she did remote meetings with the client, and that convinced her that she could do a good job meeting her clients' needs remotely. When she asked to work remotely, the ad agency refused her request. That prompted her to seek employment that would let her work and travel anywhere. For example, she spent four weeks in Santa Fiora, Italy, which is home to fewer than three thousand people. In each place she traveled, Cook would spend about three weeks working and one week being a tourist. "I loved the ability to have lived that way for four years. It was an incredible gift,"[13] she says.

## Quitting When Remote Work Is Not an Option

Cook has since decided to settle down and travel less, but she knows she could reverse course if she wanted. Researchers have found that most people who try remote work like it, as did Cook. When Owl Labs surveyed more than twenty-three hundred full-time employees in the United States for its *State of Remote Work 2022* report, soliciting opinions from employees ranging in age from their teens to their sixties, 66 percent of respondents said they would start looking for another job if they no longer had the option to work remotely. Some felt even more strongly about losing that option: 39 percent said that if they were not able to work remotely anymore, they would quit their jobs.

Christian Hänsel of Lemgo, Germany, did exactly that. Told he needed to return to the office after working remotely, the search engine optimization manager, whose job involves increasing traffic to website pages, balked. Hänsel found another position within days, then resigned. He says, "I did not feel valued as a team member. I did not feel valued as an employee and I certainly did not feel like I was being taken care of." And he advised other people to be thoughtful about whether they wanted to work in the office or remotely, concluding, "You have to stand your ground, you have to talk about it, you have to be vocal, but you also have to calculate the advantages and disadvantages to working remotely and working at the office. And you have to find out what is right for you."[14]

> "You have to stand your ground, you have to talk about it, you have to be vocal, but you also have to calculate the advantages and disadvantages to working remotely and working at the office. And you have to find out what is right for you."[14]
>
> —Christian Hänsel, remote worker based in Germany

## Productivity

Determining what is right works both ways, for employees and employers alike—and remote work offers advantages that appeal to both, starting with productivity. One of the reasons that remote work arrangements failed to catch on with employers until fairly recently was the widely held belief that if employers could not observe what workers were doing, employees would slack off. Studies have now shown that this premise is false.

In fact, employees working away from the eyes of their bosses are likely to work more rather than less. Some studies indicate that people in remote jobs put in two more hours a day than their office-bound peers. One of those studies was the Owl Labs *State of Remote Work 2021* report.

Jeff Maggioncalda, the chief executive of an online learning platform called Coursera, used to be among those executives who were dismissive of remote work. He says, "Before the pandemic, I was an old-fashioned CEO. I was a 'go to work every day' person and we used to allow some people to work from home on Wednesdays and honestly, I despised that policy. I thought, you know, if you're not coming in you're not getting the work done."[15]

Now Maggioncalda recognizes that employees can be more productive when they do not have commutes that cause them to be stuck in traffic or sitting idly on buses or trains. He also believes employers will not be able to retain their best people if they do not offer the remote option. He says, "The best talent is going to say—you want me to work for you? Here's what I need. I need flexibility. I need good pay. But part of that means I want to have a hybrid [part in-house, part remote] work experience. And those employers that don't offer hybrid, I think they're going to lose talent to those employers that do."[16]

> "The best talent is going to say—you want me to work for you? Here's what I need. I need flexibility. I need good pay. But part of that means I want to have a hybrid [part in-house, part remote] work experience. And those employers that don't offer hybrid, I think they're going to lose talent to those employers that do."[16]
>
> —Jeff Maggioncalda, chief executive of Coursera

## What Employees Want

Certainly, it is important for companies to have as much information as possible about what employees think about work so that they can base their decisions on hard data and not mere instinct. One company with its finger on the pulse of remote workers is Buffer, a social media management platform that produces an-

## The Best-Paying Flexible Jobs

The website FlexJobs, which links job hunters with remote jobs, lists the highest-paying jobs that can be done remotely. Each position requires the job holder to manage something and be experienced in his or her field. These jobs include the following:

**Medical and health services manager:** Medical and health services managers provide business services to health care providers, such as hospitals, to help them be more profitable. The average salary is about $101,000, and the number of new positions in the field is growing much faster than the average of all occupations. This position requires a bachelor's degree and in some cases a master's degree.

**Human resources manager:** In this job, which is expected to have average growth prospects in the next ten years, people help companies find and retain the right employees and act as a link between the company and its employees. The median salary for this job—with half of people making more and half making less—is $126,000. The job requires at least a bachelor's degree in business, human resources, or communications.

**Marketing manager:** People who hold this position often have degrees in journalism, advertising, or communications, all skills that come in handy when someone is in charge of communicating an organization's message to its customers and the public. A marketing manager's average salary is about $142,000. A bachelor's degree in business administration with a concentration in human resources is one possible path.

---

nual reports on the state of remote work. In 2022 Buffer surveyed more than two thousand employees and freelancers—people who work for multiple clients but are self-employed, such as writers, photographers, web designers, and journalists—in sixteen countries to learn about their attitudes regarding remote work. When they asked people what they liked most about working remotely, 67 percent said remote work allowed them more control over how they spent their time, while 62 percent gave the thumbs-up to greater flexibility. Fifty-nine percent cited having more time for themselves, 55 percent appreciated having more control over where they lived, and 44 percent agreed that they were better able to focus on work due to fewer distractions.

These responses demonstrate that remote work can allow employees to make more choices about how their day is spent. This increased freedom can potentially lead to greater balance between a person's work and personal lives. As Jessica Powell, a former vice president at Google, says:

> With our offices gone, our days have now opened up. Why *not* make that doctor's appointment for 4 p.m.? Why *not* pick the kids up at day care rather than find a babysitter? Why not try something entirely new, like going for a walk in the middle of the day, or participating in social activism or a protest during typical work hours. . . . I know I split my day differently now, sometimes having lunch with my husband and kids at noon, or starting work much earlier or later depending on what I need to get done that day.[17]

## Hiring Flexibility

As Powell knows, greater choices are not only the province of employees. They also extend to corporations. Businesses that allow their employees to work remotely are not limited to hiring people who live in the same geographic area. They can recruit people from all over the world if they are so inclined, and in doing so they can choose from a wider pool of candidates.

That certainly has been true for Ancestry.com, a Provo, Utah–based genealogical company that provides research tools for people who want to learn more about their family history. Provo often pops up on lists of the most desirable places to live, a distinction it earns from its preponderance of moun-

> "With our offices gone, our days have now opened up. Why *not* make that doctor's appointment for 4 p.m.? Why *not* pick the kids up at day care rather than find a babysitter? Why not try something entirely new, like going for a walk in the middle of the day, or participating in social activism or a protest during typical work hours."[17]
>
> —Jessica Powell, former Google vice president

## The Gift of More Time

Adults who work—particularly those with young children or older, ailing parents—are often pulled in many directions. For them, the ability to work remotely lets them use the time they save from commuting for other purposes.

The National Bureau of Economic Research—an American nonprofit research organization devoted to economic topics—released a research paper titled "Time Savings When Working from Home" that contains data gathered from employees in nearly thirty countries. Among the report's findings was that the average employee gained about two hours a week by working remotely during the pandemic. It also determined that 40 percent of this "extra" time was being put back into the performance of employees' jobs and in some cases was being funneled to a second, part-time job. Eleven percent of the added time was devoted to caregiving for children or other loved ones.

People in China reported saving the most time, 102 minutes a day, when their commutes were eliminated, followed by those in Japan, 100 minutes, and India, 99. Employees in the United States saved an average of 55 minutes a day and split that saved time this way: 42 percent to a primary or secondary job, 35 percent to doing something relaxing, and 8 percent to caregiving.

---

tains, lakes, hiking trails, and proximity to Brigham Young University. Nevertheless, Ancestry.com has found that even though persuading prospective employees to relocate to Provo is not all that difficult, it still prefers to hire top people who can work from anywhere. "By no longer being limited to the boundaries of our office locations, we can broaden our hiring capabilities to reach more under-represented talent and provide a level playing field for equitable participation of talent,"[18] says Shane Koller, the company's senior vice president of people and places. Koller's unusual job title is indicative of his company's evolution. In a memo to employees, he wrote: "Ancestry remains committed to choice and flexibility when it comes to where our employees work. . . . This means that they can continue to work from home, in the office, or a hybrid of both."[19]

## Employee Savings

While flexibility is important to both employers and employees, another priority is anything that saves time or money. Remote work can do both. Jessica Howington, a senior content manager for FlexJobs, a website that links job hunters with remote jobs, points out that monetary savings can be considerable. Howington says full-time remote workers can save as much as $12,000 a year, while hybrids—people who commute for a portion of their workweek—may save as much as $6,000 a year.

It is easy to see how savings could add up for remote workers, considering things those employees will no longer have to pay for or may pay less for. Commuting costs will plummet whether a remote worker owns a car or takes public transportation. Drivers will be putting fewer miles on their cars, which potentially translates into fewer auto repairs, lower car insurance premiums, and less money spent on gasoline. Eliminating commutes could mean a savings of $1,200 a year on gas or from $700 to $1,900 for public transportation, according to Howington.

Then there are food costs. While on the job, many people eat their lunch at restaurants. Of course, they could bring their lunch from home, but many do not. The credit card company Visa has determined that the average person spends $53 a week on lunches, which adds up to more than $2,700 in a year—money that could be saved if remote workers find it easier to make quick meals at home instead of regularly indulging in higher-priced restaurant meals.

Employees can also save money by not having to constantly update their wardrobe or pay for dry cleaning services to keep them looking nice, because remote workers usually have the freedom to dress casually. Howington estimates that the average annual household cost for clothing is about $1,400. That figure reflects business attire for men and women as well as other clothing purchases. Therefore, eliminating those costs would be akin to receiving a raise of a similar amount without employers having to provide one.

Casual dress is a major benefit of remote work. Not only are workers more comfortable, they save money they would otherwise spend on dry cleaning and wardrobe updates.

## Employer Savings

While employers may care less about ways work schedules could save their employees money, they do care a great deal about what will bolster their own bottom lines. Remote and hybrid arrangements provide cost savings to companies, making them leaner and more competitive. Global Workplace Analytics, a consulting company whose research is used by organizations that wish to optimize flexible and distributed (fully remote) work strategies, says the average US employer could save $11,000 a year on each employee it allows to work remotely 50 percent of the time. Global Workplace Analytics derives that figure from adding up the savings companies would be expected to experience through increased productivity, lower real estate costs, reduced absenteeism, and greater employee retention.

A great deal of savings can result from scaling down or eliminating office space, which results in lower real estate taxes and fewer operational and maintenance costs. Companies save money by not having to lease and equip a lot of office space, which can cost as much as $14,800 a year per employee, according to Abintra Consulting, a workplace consultancy company. And they can eliminate maintenance expenses such as hiring a plumber when the sinks in the executive washroom start dripping and employing workers to empty the trash, dust desks, vacuum floors, or perform other housekeeping services.

## Environmental Impact

In addition to curbing costs that can be measured in dollars and cents, eliminating commutes, and cutting back on everything that goes along with maintaining offices, remote work has the potential to improve the environment—although this is true only if enough people engage in it.

A global environmental challenge is climate change, which is concerning because it is thought to be responsible for intensifying weather events such as hurricanes, floods, and droughts, and because a changing climate threatens the habitats of plants, fish, and animals. One culprit causing climate change is greenhouse gas emissions. These greenhouse gases are produced when fossil fuels are burned, such as in the gasoline-powered engines that drive most automobiles.

During the COVID-19 pandemic, when people drove less, greenhouse gas emissions fell 4.6 percent worldwide in 2020. As the pandemic has eased and people have resumed moving about as they did before, greenhouse gas emissions have gone up again. According to Global Workplace Analytics' research, if everyone capable of working remotely were able to do so for half their workweek, it might be possible to reduce greenhouse emissions by 54 million tons (49 million metric tons) a year.

## Multiple Advantages to Recommend It

Whether viewed from the standpoint of the environment, corporations, or employees, remote work has much to offer. Its advantages include monetary savings, greater flexibility, the ability to work and attract employees from anywhere, and increased productivity and happiness.

*Telecommuters cite the lack of in-person meetings and micromanaging bosses as two of their favorite things about remote work.*

A senior software engineer summed up the appeal of remote work this way on Reddit, an anonymous public comment site that encourages opinions about all sorts of issues. He said, "I went from a 1.5-hour commute to 10 seconds. The lack of over-your-shoulderness is all really, really nice. I get my work done and pretty much am never bothered. That might depend on your manager though, as mine was like that even when I was in the office. Not having meetings ever is also nice, as people only tend to include you [remotely] when it's necessary."[20] With its relatively newfound acceptance and considerable advantages, remote work and its hybrid cousin are sticking around, even though the world is no longer in lockdown.

## CHAPTER THREE

# What Are the Disadvantages of Remote Work?

In 2022 Hannah Reilly graduated from Claremont McKenna College in Claremont, California, with a bachelor's degree in international relations and public policy. Seeking a position in communications, she received three job offers: two were for fully remote positions, and the third was an in-office job. She chose the in-person one, joining Verkada, a San Mateo, California, software company, as a communications consultant. Communications consultants like Reilly assist corporations with the messages they want to convey to their customers and the public.

The way Reilly saw it, working in an office would be more satisfying than working from home. During the pandemic, she disliked having to keep her distance from friends, relatives, and other people. She also viewed moving to San Mateo as a positive, looking forward to meeting new people and having new adventures there.

Reilly is happy with her decision. She relishes showing up every morning to her well-appointed office space that

> "I don't think I'd ever go back to a fully remote company at this point. Now we have all these opportunities we missed out on for so long."[21]
>
> —Hannah Reilly, Verkada in-person employee

has an in-house barista and barber. The company also provides catered meals and plenty of opportunities for employees to get to know each other.

Reilly even convinced her new roommate to apply to the company so they could commute together. "I don't think I'd ever go back to a fully remote company at this point," says Reilly, who had done some remote work as an intern—typically a part-time position held by a college student, giving that student an opportunity to learn in a professional environment. "Now we have all these opportunities we missed out on for so long."[21]

### Feelings of Missing Out

After having experienced remote work, Reilly has come to realize that it lacks some of the benefits that in-person work has to offer, such as sharing lunch with coworkers in the cafeteria, chatting at the water dispenser, and popping into a colleague's cubicle to ask a question or seek an opinion. That is why Nicole D. Smith, editorial audience director for the magazine *Harvard Business Review* (*HBR*), confessed to having mixed feelings about working remotely.

While Smith likes not having to spend nearly three hours a day commuting to her former job and believes she is thriving in her remote position, she has some fears of missing out by not being in the office with colleagues who are always there. She says:

> While my other teammates and I have been on a relatively level playing field up until this point in terms of working remotely, they have now returned to work. They're reconnecting in "real life" as I wave from the sidelines. No coffee-room morning chatter for me. No teammates stopping at my desk to say hello. No lunch breaks at the cafeteria on

the second floor of *HBR*'s office building (which I've heard of, but never visited myself). It's just going to be me: a single [person] working and living alone. A part of me can feel FOMO [fear of missing out] creeping in. Will I be excluded from private conversations that matter? . . . Will I be seen as an "other"?[22]

## Fewer Opportunities to Grow

What Smith frets about is a legitimate fear. Being remote may make it more difficult for employees to learn new skills and advance in a company. Not being present in body can lead to invisibility and being overlooked.

One senior software engineer who went from working in the office to working fully remote had this to say: "You learn much

*Some remote workers miss the camaraderie of connecting with coworkers over lunch or at after-work events.*

> "Before I moved [to full remote], I felt a lot more included in discussions in regards to everything. Now I get very surprised by things, because I'm never involved in any of the conversations that happen outside of our messaging system."[23]
>
> —Anonymous senior software engineer

less being full remote and unless your company is very good with remote employees, you're not part of any conversations. Before I moved [to full remote], I felt a lot more included in discussions in regards to everything. Now I get very surprised by things, because I'm never involved in any of the conversations that happen outside of our messaging system."[23]

Being able to learn new skills is particularly important for those at the beginning of their careers, like Reilly. Young workers can especially benefit from having mentors—a more experienced person in the company who can answer questions and take an interest in how they are doing.

For that reason, a fully remote position may not be the best choice for a first job. According to the Owl Labs *State of Remote Work 2022* report, half of the respondents to its survey agreed that managers view remote workers as less hardworking and less trustworthy than office workers, a perception that could lead to less consideration when it comes time to promote someone from within the ranks. Ironically, the 2021 Owl Labs report on remote workers found that 30 percent of men and 20 percent of women who responded to its survey said they put in more than two extra hours a week than when they worked on-site.

## Burnout, Disengagement, and Loneliness

Working too much can lead to burnout, the psychological state in which a person no longer enjoys and sometimes is incapable of performing tasks he or she once enjoyed. Burnout and disengagement—not caring about or feeling distant from their job—are not unique to remote workers, as people who work in traditional locations also face those problems. Still, what is unique about remote workers, particularly those who work at home, is that it is easy to work around the clock when all the tools of work are present at all times of the day and night. Says Gleb Tsipursky, an expert on hybrid and remote work:

> Some people expect their Slack or Microsoft Teams messages to be answered within an hour, while others check Slack once a day. Some believe email requires a response within three hours, and others feel three days is fine. As a result of such uncertainty and lack of clarity about what's appropriate, too many people feel uncomfortable disconnecting and not replying to messages or doing work tasks after hours. That might stem from a fear of not meeting their boss's expectations or not wanting to let their colleagues down.[24]

## Remote Scams

Alex Edmonds was looking for a remote job and found a digital marketing position for an apparel company that paid thirty dollars an hour. He interviewed for the job by text, never even seeing anyone from the company. He was told he had the job. There was only one problem: there was no job, only some scammer trying to get Edmonds's bank information to steal money from him.

As remote work became more popular, so too did scammers trying to swindle people seeking remote opportunities. Often, these scammers do so by borrowing the names of legitimate companies, and even real people who work at them, to trick job hunters into providing their banking information. That Edmonds never saw his interviewer face-to-face or even via Zoom was a red flag—and fortunately, it was one he recognized. He did not supply the scammer with his banking information.

According to the Federal Trade Commission, the agency responsible for policing consumer fraud, such scams have tripled since 2019. Kati Daffan, assistant director of the agency, says, "Scammers always follow the headlines and are looking to exploit the things that people need in any given moment. So we saw a lot of offers—that people could work from home, that people could have flexible jobs, that people could make a lot of money without too much effort."

Quoted in Jaime Ding, "Fake Job Scams Are Skyrocketing Online—and They Are Getting Harder to Detect," *Los Angeles Times*, January 12, 2023. www.latimes.com.

> "Some believe email requires a response within three hours, and others feel three days is fine. As a result of such uncertainty and lack of clarity about what's appropriate, too many people feel uncomfortable disconnecting and not replying to messages or doing work tasks after hours. That might stem from a fear of not meeting their boss's expectations or not wanting to let their colleagues down."[24]
>
> —Gleb Tsipursky, remote work expert

Tsipursky says that companies can help their remote employees set reasonable work-life boundaries by clearly stating policies on how long they can wait to answer email, Slack, and Microsoft Teams messages. These policies could also define the circumstances that would require a faster-than-average reply because they represent an emergency.

Moreover, remote workers may be less likely to take vacations. A full 55 percent of remote workers said they use fifteen or fewer vacation days a year, with 6 percent admitting that they took just five days off, according to the Buffer *State of Remote Work 2018* report, which measured attitudes about remote work held by employees from around the world. Vacations offer people an opportunity to take a break from work so that they feel refreshed upon returning to their usual work routine when they are done.

The same report found that 21 percent of remote workers admitted that they are lonely, and 21 percent said they find collaborating and communicating remotely with coworkers difficult. In addition, 16 percent said they were easily distracted while working from home, and 14 percent said they sometimes felt unmotivated.

## Remote Is Not Right for Everyone

For those who struggle with loneliness, disengagement, and lack of motivation, working from home might be disastrous. Among them are people who need the presence of other people to be happy—so-called extroverts who feed off their colleagues' energy—as well as employees who have a hard time resisting distractions that can occur when work and home lives blend.

Smith has developed a list of questions that can help someone decide whether he or she has the right personality to be happy as a remote worker. She suggests that people who know they are not good at organizing their time forgo the opportunity for remote work. So too should individuals who need other people around to keep them focused on the tasks at hand or who find technology vexing.

### Easier to Quit and Fire

Just as some office workers do, remote workers can feel disconnected from work and colleagues. That disconnect can make them more prone to quitting—and getting fired. "We talk to clients every day [who] are saying, 'Our employees feel disconnected, disengaged, they're not attached to our culture. They are quitting at unprecedented rates because we have people

When a person works at home, they basically never leave their office. They may have difficulty unplugging after official work hours end.

that have worked for us for two years who have never been to our office, so they're not attached to our culture . . . so they just send us an email and quit,"[25] says Nick Gianoulis. Gianoulis is the founder and co-owner of the Fun Dept., a training and development company that helps businesses form tighter bonds among their workers by hosting entertaining events.

Jessica Powell, a former vice president at Google and a business book author, has suggested that remote workers may be at greater risk of being fired because it is easier to terminate the employment of someone who is not in the same room. She says:

> For their part, employers could increasingly view their staffs as little more than interchangeable work units. As a manager, no matter how objective I think I may be, I would probably find it easier to fire an employee with whom I had little personal connection. That difficult conversation would be reduced to a few minutes on a screen, with no chance of running into the person later in the coffee room.[26]

Bosses and employees may develop closer relationships when they see each other all day. That can give the boss a better insight into the employee's personality and a greater understanding of that person's challenges and how to fix them, rather than simply regarding that employee as a face on a Zoom screen.

While it might be easier for a manager to fire or lay off a remote worker, it may be harder for the recipient to receive the bad news when it is delivered via Zoom, Slack, or email, sometimes in the middle of the night. Kerensa Cadenas found that to be true when she read an email informing her of a layoff. At the time, the thirty-seven-year-old was sitting alone in her apartment and mused that she missed the comfort of commiserating with colleagues. As it turned out, she was among one hundred coworkers at Vox Media who had lost their jobs, and she was immediately beset by worries.

Workers who are nothing more to each other than faces on a Zoom screen may not feel as connected as in-person coworkers do.

She says, "It's scary because I'm like: Will I ever have a savings account? Am I ever going to own something? Probably not."[27]

While never pleasant, layoffs experienced by remote workers can be even more traumatizing, as companies may not be doing enough to help their laid-off employees find new jobs. When they are let go, employees cannot simply walk into the human resources department and ask for assistance. In addition to hiring and training, human resources departments also can provide resources such as résumé advice and career counseling for employees who unexpectedly have to sever their relationship with the company.

### Remote Software: Monitoring or Spying?

It is perhaps ironic that remote employees who are not within physical sight of their employers may nonetheless find themselves undergoing intrusive scrutiny through the installation of software that lets employers monitor their productivity. This software may be capable of detecting when an employee has begun or stopped work and even monitoring his or her emails. As long as the employee is using a company computer, such monitoring is legal and is not something that employers even need to tell employees about. Still, it brings up privacy concerns. Thorin Klosowski, a journalist who writes about privacy and security issues, says,

> The data generated from what a worker does throughout the day, whether it's anonymized or not, represents a privacy concern, and it's easy to imagine scenarios in which an employer might use that data impractically or unethically. Since bossware [a general term for software tools that monitor employees] take periodic screenshots or record video—sometimes without an employee knowing—the software may incidentally pick up all sorts of sensitive information, such as medical or banking information.[28]

## Improving Video Calls

According to Owl Labs' *State of Remote Work 2021* report, video calls between people in the office and remote workers do not always work well, with 70 percent of respondents reporting difficulties. Problems cited range from not being able to tell who is speaking to not being able to read body language and facial expressions and feeling disengaged from the discussion.

Businesses who invest in technology developed for hybrid workplaces could mitigate those problems. However, Owl Labs found that fewer than 40 percent of its survey respondents said their employers had made such upgrades. Kate Lister, president of Global Workplace Analytics, whose research produced the Owl Labs report, says, "Make no mistake, fully remote is easier than hybrid. We've grown accustomed to all being equal squares on a screen. It's made the whole work experience more egalitarian, but when some people are in the room and some are not, we will need to be very intentional about making sure everyone's voice is heard and everyone is measured by what they do rather than where they do it."

Quoted in Brianna Crandall, "State of Remote Work Report Reveals Employees Want Hybrid Work More than Employers Do," FMLink, December 1, 2021. www.fmlink.com.

Karlee Besse, an accountant in British Columbia, Canada, was fired from a company and asked to return wages she earned through "time theft." Besse knew that her work computer had a program called TimeCamp installed on it that could identify when she was doing company work versus personal tasks. Her employer determined that she had billed for fifty-one hours of work that she did not do, according to the tracking software. In addition to losing her job, Besse was asked to return the money she received under allegedly false pretenses. Believing she was in the right, Besse countersued the company but lost in the Canadian court system. She was required to pay her former employer $1,500 in wages she was paid before her transgression was discovered. Besse admitted that she found the software hard to use and had trouble getting it to distinguish which tasks were work-related and which were personal. Still, she acknowledged, "I've plugged time to files that I didn't touch and that wasn't right or appropriate in any way or fashion, and I recognize that and so for that I'm really sorry."[29]

## Rising Costs

Of course, it is a rare occurrence when employees have to return the money they have earned to their employers. Less rare, however, is the fact that working from home may place some financial burdens normally assumed by companies on the shoulders of remote workers. For example, when workers spend more time at home, their energy bills tend to go up as they pay more to heat or cool their residence. In a recent survey of one thousand respondents, Sky Connect, a provider of Wi-Fi services to businesses, found that at least half of those surveyed were avoiding working from home in order to save money on their rising energy bills. For comfort's sake, they used coworking spaces, cafés, and public libraries, where they could be warm.

Stacey Hill, director of sales and operations at Sky Connect, says, "The cost-of-living crisis is a huge concern for consumers and small businesses alike. But for those spending the most time at home, increasing energy bills are understandably putting a strain on personal finances."[30]

In addition to energy costs, remote workers may have to pay for internet services that are free at the office. For instance, a survey conducted by Buffer found that 75 percent of respondents were not reimbursed for their home internet fees, and 71 percent of those who used coworking spaces said their employers did not reimburse them for those costs.

Despite its many advantages, remote work also has some less desirable aspects: more costs being borne by employees, feelings of disconnection and burnout, and lost promotion and mentoring possibilities among them. Over time, thoughtful companies that care about retaining their workers will likely learn to mitigate those downsides.

## CHAPTER FOUR

# What Will the Future of Remote Work Look Like?

In May 2023 President Joe Biden declared the COVID-19 pandemic officially over. Yet the changes the pandemic wrought in the workplace and the lives of employees laboring there are likely to continue.

Many employees who had the chance to work remotely appreciated the freedom they experienced and did not want to give it up. Corporations realized that remote employees could be as productive as in-house staff. Still, some corporations began asking their workers to come back full time or for at least a few days a week—with employees sometimes expressing their displeasure about having to do so.

### Pushing Back

At the Walt Disney Company—whose employees work for entities such as the ABC TV network, the Hulu streaming service, and the film studios 20th Century, Marvel, and Pixar—employees resisted the call to return to the office four days a week. The new policy had blindsided them after they had become used to working in the office only two or three days

> "I know it's a hassle to come to the office. But if you're just sitting in your pajamas in your bedroom, is that the work life you want to live? ... If we don't feel like we're part of something important, what's the point? If it's just a paycheck, then what have you reduced your life to?"[33]
>
> —Malcolm Gladwell, best-selling author

a week. More than twenty-three hundred Disney employees petitioned management to reverse course. Among the points they made in the petition was: "This policy will slow, or even reverse, our post-COVID recovery and growth by creating critical resource shortages and causing irreplaceable institutional knowledge loss."[31]

The petition suggested that many employees would resign rather than be forced back into the office. As one employee said, "Flexibility at Disney really felt like a fresh start. Now it feels like we're moving backward."[32] Management saw it differently, arguing that more face time would benefit creativity, corporate culture, and, ultimately, Disney employees' careers.

Some experts support Disney, as well as other companies—including Starbucks, Amazon, and Google—in making their employees return to pre-pandemic work habits. Malcolm Gladwell is among them. The best-selling author, whom *Time* magazine has singled out as one of the most influential people in the world, says, "It's not in your best interest to work at home. I know it's a hassle to come to the office. But if you're just sitting in your pajamas in your bedroom, is that the work life you want to live? ... If we don't feel like we're part of something important, what's the point? If it's just a paycheck, then what have you reduced your life to?"[33]

### Making Hybrid Arrangements Work

While Disney, Starbucks, automaker Tesla, and other companies have been trying to get their workers back in person, other companies are trying to make hybrid schedules work for them by refining the concept. Among them is RingCentral, which provides businesses with more efficient ways to call, message, and meet with their customers and employees. Based in Belmont, California, the tech company had been asking employees to come into the office three days a week before it made a change: it asked employees to come into the office thirty days in a quarter, letting them choose where those days would fall. Under this arrangement, in any three-month period, employees could elect to work from home for weeks at a time if it suited their needs. Mo Katibeh, RingCentral's chief operating officer, says, "Really it's about flexibility and accountability."[34]

Some hybrid arrangements allow employees to use coworking spaces. The same is also true for fully distributed companies in which everyone is remote. For the most part, fully distributed companies are high-tech companies. Automatic is an example. The web development company, which employs twelve hundred

Due to the ending of the COVID-19 pandemic, Google and some other major companies have required employees to return to the office. Some employees are resisting this change.

people in seventy-five countries, sold its expensive headquarters in San Francisco, replacing it with a smaller space for holding board meetings and a coworking space in New York.

## Simplifying Information

In addition to using coworking spaces, Automatic has centralized the way employees receive information, making it available without the need to communicate with many different individuals. While it is easy enough to ask questions of colleagues when working in person, trying to get information from colleagues who are working remotely can be more challenging. So Automatic and other companies have decided to address the special challenges that remote workers face head-on. For example, Automatic relies on company blogs to impart important information, requiring its managers to post updates promptly so that the people they manage can make use of it.

DuckDuckGo, a fully distributed search engine company, has also simplified how it communicates with its one hundred employees in seventeen countries. DuckDuckGo uses a software program to put the information employees need to know most in front of their eyes. Then it has them limit their work to one single important project at a time that only a few people are working on. To avoid complications and the need to consult multiple colleagues, it gives them a guide containing everything they need to know to complete an assignment.

DuckDuckGo is also addressing the important needs remote workers have, from outfitting their offices to reducing loneliness. It offers everything from a $500 stipend per month to use a coworking space to reimbursements for new desks, computers, and smartphones every couple of years.

To encourage social time, DuckDuckGo asks employees to participate in virtual meetups with four people they do not usually work with. It lets them take "work-cations" with colleagues in appealing destinations around the world. A work-cation com-

On a "work-cation," employees travel to locations where they work part of the time, but take time to enjoy vacation activities as well. Work styles are usually more casual than in an office.

bines work with vacation downtime. There is also an annual company retreat, and each quarter, people are given an opportunity to work on whatever project they want. DuckDuckGo has embraced the concept that what is good for its employees is good for the company.

## Developing Virtual Offices

Another approach to making remote work more user-friendly is the development of virtual offices that simulate some of the features of brick-and-mortar offices but exist only on computer screens. One start-up company that is developing a virtual office platform is Branch, headed by a CEO who is not yet even twenty. His name is Dayton Mills, and he lives in Seattle, Washington. Mills has been interested in computers since his middle school days, when he enjoyed playing *Minecraft*, a video game that lets players build virtual worlds and has been described as a computerized version of LEGO sets. Mills is developing a virtual office that may one day bridge the gap between an in-person office and an online office. One person described a visit to Branch's virtual office this way:

> When you log into an office, you become a colorful, smiley-face blob. You have a bird's eye view of the entire office and can guide your avatar around the different rooms, all of which are customizable. There are conference rooms, cafeterias, private offices, breakout rooms, game rooms, and even the dreaded copier/mail room makes an appearance. You can toggle your webcam on or off as you please. Once it's on, your face will appear in a little circular frame at the top of the screen, along with anyone who is within earshot. It feels a bit like corporate *Pokemon* or an early version of *Zelda* if the purpose of the game were to survive a conference call.[35]

## The Future of Unions

As employees who once worked remotely are asked to return to the office, there may be some unintended consequences. One of those consequences may be encouraging employees to unionize.

Labor unions are organizations created to represent the interests of employees in specific industries to management. Members pay dues, elect representatives to negotiate on their behalf, and have the right to vote on labor contracts. As many as one in three American workers were in a union in the 1950s. Today that figure is one in ten.

There are signs, however, that union membership is being revitalized. In August 2022 the polling company Gallup released its Work and Education Survey. It found that approval of unions is at its highest level since 1965, 71 percent. In 2022 employees at 260 Starbucks locations, for example, voted to join a union.

Gleb Tsipursky, an expert on remote and hybrid work, says, "By ignoring the benefits of remote work and forcing their employees back to the office, employers risk alienating their workers, and they may also be creating a situation where workers are more likely to unionize. This is because when employees feel that their needs are not being met, they are more likely to band together and form a union to protect their interests."

Gleb Tsipursky, "Why Employers Forcing a Return to Work Is Leading to More Worker Power and Unionization," *Entrepreneur*, February 22, 2023. www.entrepreneur.com.

People who work in the virtual office and their avatars can speak to each other should they find themselves hanging out in the same part of the virtual office setup. The closer a person gets to a colleague, the louder that colleague's voice sounds. As the person wanders away from that colleague, the voice gets softer, just as it would in real life. One person who tried the platform says, "It's easy to dismiss the effect as a gimmick, but the effect is curiously disarming, maybe even a bit profound."[36]

## Workplace Holograms

In addition to virtual offices developed to make working remotely more like working in person, other means are being tapped to make attending meetings virtually a bit more like being present in person. One of the criticisms people have of attending virtual meetings when others are physically in the meeting room is that they feel disconnected and ignored. A solution would be a way to remain at home and yet be present in a distance meeting at the same time.

Workplace holograms could make it so. A hologram is a 3-D digital image that looks so lifelike that it is easy to believe that the image represents a flesh-and-blood person in the same room.

Were holograms as widely available in the workplace as they are in movies, for example, a remote employee could project his or her image into a meeting, conference call, or interview, thereby having the same advantages as anyone else who is in the room. While this may sound fantastical, the technology for creating holograms is being developed by multiple companies. Two of the larger players in the field are Google and Microsoft. Microsoft's Mesh lets people project a virtual version of themselves that mimics their facial expressions and body movements. Google is working on Project Starline, which uses 3-D imagery that is compressed and displayed in such a way that makes the image appear real and in the room. "Hologram technology is advancing extremely fast, and with more companies and businesses developing their methods of communication, we can expect this technology to

*Holograms are 3-D images. Someday, people may participate as holograms in meetings when they cannot be physically present.*

become even more mainstream over the next few years,"[37] says Compass Offices, a supplier of office spaces to companies in many countries, including Australia, China, Japan, and Vietnam.

## Personality Testing

Holograms are a fun new technology that may change the future of work. They are a tool that can bridge the gap between those in the office and those working from home. Another tool that companies are already finding useful in connection to remote work is personality testing, which is being used to change the way people are hired.

Now that work has so many options—full-time in-person, hybrid, remote—companies may want to know whether people they are considering hiring will work best in the office or on their own. One of the ways they are doing this is through personality testing. After all, it costs money to put people in a job that is a poor fit for them and could lead to that person being unhappy and quitting in short order, necessitating that the hiring process be started all over again to find a replacement.

Toronto-based company Scotiabank relies on personality tests to fill the ranks of its ninety thousand employees. In fact, the company says it finds such tests more important than what is on an applicant's résumé, particularly when a job candidate has just finished college. Scotiabank reports that its reliance on personality testing has thus far led to a more diverse workforce. Women now make up half of its hires, and the percentage of Black employees has risen from 1 percent to 6 percent.

Among other things, personality tests can reveal who is likely to thrive working remotely, who is a team player and enjoys collaboration, who is perfectly happy working independently with little supervision, and who prefers variety to spending every day the same way.

Caitlin MacGregor, the cofounder of a research-backed testing company called Plum, says that tests like those her company offers can help spot potential employees' natural abilities they may not yet have had a chance to use. "For a long time, people were comfortable making decisions around talent based on face-to-face interactions," she says. "More and more companies have a distributed workforce. It's harder than ever to get to know your people."[38] Personality testing can provide the missing information.

### Emergence of a Four-Day Workweek

While future workers will be able to apply for jobs that suit their preferred way to work—remote, hybrid, or fully office based—they will also have an opportunity to decide when to work. The popularity of remote and hybrid work has already led to a decline in the typical nine-to-five workday that used to be a given in most jobs. It is certainly possible that this increased flexibility may also lead to more people being able to experience a four-day workweek.

Experiments with four days of work followed by three days of leisure have been going on for some time, and research has determined that not only do employees embrace the concept, they also get more done, experience less stress, and enjoy enhanced feelings of well-being. For example, when Microsoft gave a four-day workweek a trial in Japan, company leaders were delighted by a 40 percent boost in productivity. Other countries in which the

> "Organizations should embrace the four-day week to retain staff and attract new talent. The pandemic has permanently altered how employers and employees approach their work arrangements, so calls for a four-day workweek will only grow louder."[39]
>
> —Ben Laker, professor, University of Reading's Henley Business School

government or corporations have been experimenting with a shortened workweek are Ireland and Spain.

Ben Laker, a professor at the University of Reading's Henley Business School in Great Britain, finds much to like in the four-day workweek, for employees and employers both. The latter, he says, can enhance the quality of their staff by offering such a flexible arrangement. He points out that one bank that switched to a shorter workweek saw a 500 percent increase in the number of people wanting to work for it. He says, "Organizations should embrace the four-day week to retain staff and attract new talent. The pandemic has permanently altered how employers and employees approach their work arrangements, so calls for a four-day workweek will only grow louder."[39]

## Why Coworking Spaces Work

Coworking spaces are popping up around the country. While ordinary offices are typically dedicated to a single company, coworking spaces are nicely appointed work spaces that are shared by a variety of professionals in many different fields.

People who use coworking spaces are typically asked to sign an agreement in which they promise to follow certain rules. This is important because they will be working near other people in a large room without individual offices or cubicles. They can choose to socialize and exchange ideas with the others in the space if they want to collaborate.

Individuals and corporations rent space that is accessible to them around the clock, making it easy to work whenever the mood suits them. Highly popular, these thoughtfully put-together spaces have a leg up on conventional offices when it comes to work satisfaction. They also cost less than outfitting a dedicated office.

Coworking space users say they can get their jobs done without worrying about trying to impress anyone else in the office. They say they feel freer to be who they are. And since other people are working nearby, they can get a boost from the creative energy that comes from working with other people who welcome being part of a collaborative atmosphere.

## Looking Ahead

The sudden onset of remote work due to the pandemic, and its success in keeping companies afloat during that period, became a trial balloon for what the future of work might be. It represented a seismic shift whose aftershocks continue to be felt. Those aftershocks are likely to impact the future lives of working people in ways that can only be guessed at today. There is agreement that remote work is here to stay and that hybrid arrangements will persist for the foreseeable future. As Erin Lewellen, the CEO of Global Citizen Year, a San Francisco nonprofit with fifty employees, says:

> "If you do your best work remotely and in another country, so be it. If you need the structure of an office environment, let's support that. We all feel best when equipped to do our best work, and that means different things to different people."[40]
>
> —Erin Lewellen, nonprofit CEO

> I believe we are moving into an age where no one wants work to dominate their life. Folks want work to be a part of their life, and they want work to add purpose (if possible); but regardless, they don't want it to be the focal point. We are choosing to focus on the what, not the how. If you do your best work remotely and in another country, so be it. If you need the structure of an office environment, let's support that. We all feel best when equipped to do our best work, and that means different things to different people.[40]

If there is one certainty, it is that companies that embrace change and what is best for their employees will be rewarded with employees who stay and bring the best of themselves to their jobs, whether they work from a coffee shop, their home, or the office.

# SOURCE NOTES

## Introduction: A Seismic Shift in the Workplace

1. Quoted in Larry Bernstein, *What Happens Next in 6 Minutes with Larry Bernstein*, podcast, October 8, 2022. www.whathappensnextin6minutes.com.
2. Quoted in Jane Thier, "I Proudly Wake Up at 8:59 A.M., One Minute Before Starting My Remote Job. There Are Thousands Like Me, and We Don't Care What You Think," Yahoo!, October 23, 2022. www.yahoo.com.
3. Quoted in M. Corey Goldman, "Going Back to the Office Is Toast, for Real This Time," TheStreet, January 12, 2022. www.thestreet.com.
4. Quoted in Abha Bhattari, "The Great Mismatch: Remote Work Is in Demand, but Positions Are Drying Up," *Washington Post*, November 27, 2022. www.washingtonpost.com.

## Chapter One: What Is It Like to Work from Home?

5. Stella Garber, "A Day in the Life of a Remote Worker," Medium, January 9, 2020. https://medium.com.
6. Garber, "A Day in the Life of a Remote Worker."
7. Quoted in Ed Berthiaume, "Jack Nilles Tried to Ignite a Work-from-Home Trend 48 Years Ago. It's Finally Here," Lawrence University, August 17, 2020. www.lawrence.edu.
8. Quoted in Berthiaume, "Jack Nilles Tried to Ignite a Work-from-Home Trend 48 Years Ago."
9. Frank W. Schiff, "Working at Home Can Save Gasoline," *Washington Post*, September 2, 1979. washingtonpost.com.
10. Quoted in Natalie Hamingson, "Communication Technology and Inclusion Will Shape the Future of Remote Work," Business News Daily, March 6, 2023. www.businessnewsdaily.com.
11. Tsedal Neeley, *Remote Work Revolution: Succeeding from Anywhere*. New York: Harper Business, 2021, p. 58.
12. Quoted in Berthiaume, "Jack Nilles Tried to Ignite a Work-from-Home Trend 48 Years Ago."

## Chapter Two: What Are the Advantages of Working Remotely?

13. Quoted in Jordan Pandy, "I've Worked Remotely from 15 Different Countries. Here's What I've Learned," Insider, January 27, 2023. www.businessinsider.co.za.
14. Quoted in Ian Rose, "I Quit My Job Rather than Go Back to the Office," BBC News, December 19, 2022. www.bbc.com.
15. Quoted in Rose, "I Quit My Job Rather than Go Back to the Office."
16. Quoted in Nidhi Singal, "Employers Who Don't Embrace Hybrid Will Lose Talent, Says Coursera Boss Jeff Maggioncalda," *Business Today*, October 25, 2022. www.businesstoday.in.
17. Jessica Powell, "The Rise of Remote Work Can Be Unexpectedly Liberating," *New York Times*, September 25, 2020. www.nytimes.com.
18. Quoted in Taylor Telford, "America's Offices Are Now Half-Full. They May Not Get Much Fuller," *Washington Post*, February 4, 2023. www.washingtonpost.com.
19. Shane Koller, "Shane Koller's Post," LinkedIn, 2023. www.linkedin.com.
20. Quoted in Reddit, "Remote Discussion Thread," 2019. www.reddit.com.

## Chapter Three: What Are the Disadvantages of Remote Work?

21. Quoted in Telford, "America's Offices Are Now Half-Full."
22. Nicole D. Smith, "I Have Mixed Feelings About Working Remotely Full Time," *Harvard Business Review*, November 2, 2021. https://hbr.org.
23. Quoted in Reddit, "Remote Discussion Thread."
24. Gleb Tsipursky, "Does Remote Work Hurt Wellbeing and Work-Life Balance?," *Forbes*, November 1, 2022. www.forbes.com.
25. Quoted in Lizzy McLellan Ravitch, "Having Fun at Work Can Make Your Teams More Productive—and These Experts Built a Business Around It," *Philadelphia (PA) Inquirer*, January 27, 2023. www.inquirer.com.
26. Powell, "The Rise of Remote Work Can Be Unexpectedly Liberating."
27. Quoted in Emma Goldberg, "Laid Off in Your Living Room: The Chaos of the Remote Job Cuts," *New York Times*, January 30, 2023. www.nytimes.com.
28. Thorin Klosowski, "How Your Boss Can Use Your Remote-Work Tools to Spy on You," *New York Times*, February 10, 2021. www.nytimes.com.
29. Quoted in Stephanie Stacey, "A Woman Who Claimed She Was Wrongly Dismissed Was Ordered to Repay Her Former Employer About $2,000 for Misrepresenting Her Working Hours," Insider, January 13, 2023. www.businessinsider.com.
30. Quoted in Orianna Rosa Royle, "Remote Workers and Freelancers Are Cutting Back on Working from Home—Because It's Too Expensive," Yahoo!, February 16, 2023. www.yahoo.com.

## Chapter Four: What Will the Future of Remote Work Look Like?

31. Quoted in Taylor Telford, "Return to Disney Offices Fought," *Washington Post*, February 16, 2023. www.washingtonpost.com.
32. Quoted in Telford, "Return to Disney Offices Fought."
33. Quoted in Minda Zetlin, "Malcolm Gladwell Says Remote Work Is Bad for Employees—and a Lot of People Are Mad at Him," *Inc.*, August 11, 2022. www.inc.com.
34. Quoted in Telford, "America's Offices Are Now Half-Full."
35. Charlie Warzel and Anne Helen Petersen, *Out of Office: The Big Problem and Bigger Promise of Working from Home*. New York: Knopf, 2021, p. 165.
36. Warzel and Petersen, *Out of Office*, p. 166.
37. Compass Offices, "Are Workplace Holograms the Future of Work?," April 5, 2022. www.compassoffices.com.
38. Quoted in Emma Goldberg, "The $2 Billion Question of Who You Are at Work," *New York Times*, March 5, 2023. www.nytimes.com.
39. Ben Laker, "What Does the Four-Day Workweek Mean for the Future of Work?," *MIT Sloan Management Review*, May 16, 2022. https://sloanreview.mit.edu.
40. Quoted in Mark Sullivan and Grace Buono, "What the Future of Hybrid Work Will (and Won't) Look Like, According to 27 Business Leaders," *SHRM Executive Newsletter*, August 4, 2022. www.shrm.org.

# FOR FURTHER RESEARCH

## Books

Jill Duffy, *The Everything Guide to Remote Work: The Ultimate Resource for Remote Employees, Hybrid Workers, and Digital Nomads*. Avon, MA: Adams Media, 2022.

Chris Dyer and Kim Shepherd, *Remote Work: Redesign Processes, Practices and Strategies to Engage a Remote Workforce*. New York: Kogan Page, 2021.

Lonely Planet, *The Digital Nomad Handbook*. Fort Mill, SC: Lonely Planet, 2020.

Liam Martin and Rob Rawson, *Running Remote: Master the Lessons from the World's Most Successful Remote-Work Pioneers*. Nashville, TN: Harper Collins Leadership, 2022.

Tsedal Neeley, *Remote Work Revolution: Succeeding from Anywhere*. New York: Harper Business, 2021.

Charlie Warzel and Anne Helen Petersen, *Out of Office: The Big Problem and Bigger Promise of Working from Home*. New York: Knopf, 2021.

## Internet Sources

Ed Berthiaume, "Jack Nilles Tried to Ignite a Work-from-Home Trend 48 Years Ago. It's Finally Here," Lawrence University, August 17, 2020. www.lawrence.edu.

Caterina Bulgarella, "What Wear-Your-Pajamas-to-Work Days Can Do for the Office Culture," *Forbes*, August 8, 2022. www.forbes.com.

Lydia Dishman, "The Future of Work. No, Remote Work Isn't a 'New' Perk—It's Been Around for About 1.4 Million Years," *Fast Company*, April 16, 2019. www.fastcompany.com.

Emma Goldberg, "Laid Off in Your Living Room: The Chaos of the Remote Job Cuts," *New York Times*, January 30, 2023. www.nytimes.com.

Natalie Hamingson, "Communication Technology and Inclusion Will Shape the Future of Remote Work," Business News Daily, March 6, 2023. www.businessnewsdaily.com.

Ryan Jenkins, "Malcolm Gladwell's Fears About Remote Work Are Real: It's Your Brain That's Telling You Lies—Here's Why," *Entrepreneur*, September 14, 2022. www.entrepreneur.com.

Jordan Pandy, "I've Worked Remotely from 15 Different Countries. Here's What I've Learned," Insider, January 27, 2023. www.businessinsider.co.za.

Taylor Telford, "America's Offices Are Now Half-Full. They May Not Get Much Fuller," *Washington Post*, February 4, 2023. www.washingtonpost.com.

## Websites

**Flex Jobs**
www.flexjobs.com
This website contains listings for remote jobs as well as information on the latest trends in remote jobs and answers to questions about career advancement. There are also articles that talk about what various jobs entail, what coworking spaces are, and whether remote work discrimination exists.

**Guide to Hybrid Working and Managing Remote Teams**
www.gallup.com/workplace/316313/understanding-and-managing-remote-workers.aspx
This website contains a report written by the Gallup Organization that outlines how hybrid work differs from remote work, what the best remote-work jobs are, why hybrid represents the future of work, and more.

**Remote POC**
https://remotepoc.com
Remote POC connects remote-friendly companies to job applicants of color. Its website offers advice and support opportunities and case studies of people who have found remote work jobs.

**We Work Remotely**
https://weworkremotely.com
We Work Remotely claims to be the largest remote work community, with 4.5 million visitors. This website offers access to a blog with topics of interest about remote work, as well as to episodes of the remote work podcast *The Remote Show*.

# INDEX

*Note: Boldface page numbers indicate illustrations.*

Abintra Consulting, 28
Amazon, 44
Ancestry.com, 24, 25
Automatic (web development company), 45–46

Barrero, Jose Maria, 11
Bell, Alexander Graham, 11
benefits of remote work
   balance between work/personal life and, 23–24, 25
   costs savings to employees as, 25–26
   costs savings to employers as, 12, 27–28
   environmental, 12–13, 28–29
   hiring flexibility, 24–25
   increased productivity, 15, 21–22, 28
Besse, Karlee, 41
Biden, Joe, 43
Bloom, Nicholas, 5
Buffer (social media management platform), 22–23, 42
burnout, 34, 42

Cadenas, Kerensa, 38–39
Cenedella, Marc, 6–7
Census Bureau, US, 5, 11
Cisco, 14, 15
clothing costs, 26
commuting costs, 26
Compass Offices (office space company), 49–50
conference calls. *See* video/conference calls
Cook, Rhiannon, 19–20
COVID-19 pandemic, 43
   decline in greenhouse gas emissions during, 28
   ending of remote work following, 43–44
   prevalence of remote work before versus after, 4
coworking space, 13, 45–46, 52

Daffan, Kati, 35
disabilities, remote work as boon for people with, 14
disadvantages of remote work
   burnout/disengagement as, 34–36
   ease of laying off workers/workers quitting as, 37–39
   fewer opportunities to advance/learn new skills as, 33–34
   increased costs to employees as, 41–42
   loss of face time as, 32–33, 44

disengagement, 34, 36, 37–38
Disney. *See* Walt Disney Company
DuckDuckGo (search engine company), 46–47

Edmonds, Alex, 35

Federal Trade Commission, 35
flexible jobs. *See* remote/flexible jobs
Flexiplace, 13
FlexJobs (website), 23, 26, 58
food costs, 26
four-day workweek, 51–52

Gallup poll, 48
Garber, Stella, 8–9
General Services Administration, 15
Gianoulis, Nick, 38
Gladwell, Malcolm, 44
Global Workplace Analytics, 27–29, 40
Google, 44, **45**, 49
greenhouse gas emissions, 28–29
Guide to Hybrid Working and Managing Remote Teams (website), 58

Hänsel, Christian, 21
Hill, Stacey, 41–42
hiring
    personality testing and, 50–51
    remote work and flexibility in, 24–25
holograms, 49–50, **50**
Howington, Jessica, 26
human resources managers, 17, 23, 39
hybrid arrangements, 30, 44–46, 51, 53

employer savings from, 27–28
investment in technology for, 40

IBM, 14–15

Katibeh, Mo, 45
Koller, Shane, 25

labor unions, 48
Laker, Ben, 52
Lambert, Samantha, 16–17
landlines, 11
Lewellen, Erin, 53
Lister, Kate, 40
loneliness, 36

MacGregor, Caitlin, 51
Maggioncalda, Jeff, 22
marketing manager, 23
medical/health services manager, 23
Microsoft, 36, 49, 51
Miller, Meagan, 9
Mills, Dayton, 47–48
monitoring software, 39–40

Nair, Vivek, 9–10
National Bureau of Economic Research, 25
Neeley, Tsedal, 17
Nilles, Jack, 11–12, 18

Obama, Barack, 16
office space
    coworking, 13, 45–46, 52
    reduced need for, 15, 28
opinion polls. *See* surveys
Owl Labs, 21, 22, 34

Pensack, Amanda, 5–6
Plum (testing company), 51

Pollak, Julia, 7
polls. *See* surveys
Powell, Jessica, 24, 38
privacy concerns, monitoring software and, 39–40
productivity
   remote work increases, 15, 21–22, 28, 39–40
   shortened workweek and, 51–52
   software monitoring of, 39–40
Project Starline (hologram technology), 49–50

Reddit (social media platform), 30
Reilly, Hannah, 31–32
remote/flexible jobs
   as boon for people with disabilities, 14
   federal government as early proponent of, 15–16
   first companies implementing, 14–15
   highest-paying, 23
   high-tech companies as leaders in, 14–15
   history of, 10–13
   hybrid arrangements for, 44–46
   jobs/locations not amenable to, 11, 17
   prevalence of, before versus after COVID-19 pandemic, 4
   productivity and, 15, 21–22, 28
   role of federal government in promoting, 15–16
   *See also* benefits of remote work; disadvantages of remote work
Remote POC (website), 58
RingCentral (tech company), 44–45

Schiff, Frank W., 12–13
Scotiabank, 50–51
Sky Connect (Wi-Fi provider), 41
Slack (message-sharing app), 8, 35, 36
Smith, Nicole D., 32–33, 36–37
Starbucks, 44, 48
*State of Remote Work 2018* (Buffer), 36
*State of Remote Work 2021* (Owl Labs), 22, 40
*State of Remote Work 2022* (Owl Labs), 21, 34
Sun Microsystems, 14, 15
surveys
   on approval of labor unions, 48
   on attitudes about remote work, 23
   of employers upgrading remote technology, 40
   on home working and energy bills, 41–42
   on losing option of remote work, 21
   on perception of managers' views on remote versus in-house workers, 34
   on remote work among rural populations, 11
   on vacation time taken/attitudes of remote workers, 36

telecommuting, 11
   early study on, 12
Telework Enhancement Act (2010), 16
Tesla, 44
*Time* (magazine), 44
time savings, 24, 25

"Time Savings When Working from Home" (National Bureau of Economic Research), 25
time theft, 41
Tsipursky, Gleb, 35–36, 48

vacations, 36
video/conference calls, 8, 20, **39**
   layoffs by, 38
   upgrading technology for, 40

Walt Disney Company, 43–44
We Work Remotely (website), 58
Work and Education Survey (Gallup), 48
workweek, four-day, 51–52

Zoom (videoconferencing app), 8, 38

# PICTURE CREDITS

Cover: Josep Suria/Shutterstock

6: Drazen Zigic/Shutterstock
10: Prostock-studio/Shutterstock
13: barteverett/Shutterstock
17: Just dance/Shutterstock
20: StevanZZ/Shutterstock
27: Vadym Pastukh/Shutterstock
29: Ground Picture/Shutterstock
33: Dmytro Zinkevych/Shutterstock
37: DimaBerlin/Shutterstock
39: Kateryna Onyshchuk/Shutterstock
45: Uladzik Kryhin/Shutterstock
47: David Pereiras/Shutterstock
50: Gorodenkoff/Shutterstock

## ABOUT THE AUTHOR

Gail Snyder is a freelance writer and advertising copywriter who has written more than twenty books for young readers. She lives in Chalfont, Pennsylvania, with her husband, Hal Marcovitz.